GLAM IT UP!

A SIMPLE GUIDE TO BEING YOUR OWN INTERIOR DESIGNER

Grace Annan

ISBN-13: 978-0692632093
ISBN-10: 0692632093

To Ms. Kaiser

for your unfailing love, encouragement,
and counsel.

Contents

A Word from the Author

Who says you need a professional interior designer to decorate or renovate your home? You really don't. All you need is a pinch of creativity and a drop of inspiration.

This book will guide you through the steps you need to materialize your inspiration and creative thoughts.

The Creative Process

Chapter 1

As an interior designer, I am always open to finding different sources of inspiration, which have been facilitated by mediums such as Facebook, Instagram, and Pinterest, just to name a few. I also draw inspiration from colors and unusual patterns provided by the vast cultures that our world provides. When renovating your home, or space, I always suggest trying to incorporate objects or colors that might be considered unusual to provide your environment with a "pop" that will catch the eye.

When you make the decision to decorate your home, use the technology available to us all to gather as much inspirational material, or ideas, first. The gathering of material will give you an idea of the theme you are primarily drawn to and will ease the clutter in your mind. Next, you want to reflect on your style preferences. Would you prefer a dark, cozy look or are you drawn to a simple and bright room? Maybe you like color, color and more color?

The following is a short list of some of the most popular interior design styles:

BOHEMIAN: Carefree, vibrant, and earthy. It is characterized by the use of colors and unusual, unique, ethnic, and rare décor.

RUSTIC: Warm, organic, and hearty. The primary material for this style is wood, and wood beams, which are used to frame ceilings, doors and windows, to line walls, and to surround fireplaces.

TRADITIONAL: Channels old European décor with warm wood tones, detailed furnishings, and elegant décor.

MODERN/CONTEMPORARY: Sleek, clean, open, and simple. The furniture and décor are architectural in nature with neutral colors. This style also embraces the use and ease of modern technology.

MODERN INDUSTRIAL: Features the use of raw steel, copper-tone décor with exposed brick walls.

CONTEMPORARY CHIC: Clean, fresh, and features a balance of colors and refined décor.

VINTAGE: Nostalgic, classic and charming. The design is created with antique, rusted, peeling furniture (often bought at flea markets).

ZEN: Feel of calm, air, openness and relaxation featuring natural materials, such as wood and bamboo, and low, ground-level furniture. This style is inspired by the Asian culture.

NAUTICAL: Sea or ocean feel, or simply the feel of being on vacation. It is relaxing, positive, and bright. The most popular colors are white and blue, and the décor consists of seashells, sand, and other sea elements.

ECLECTIC: Does not focus on a specific element, but a combination of styles.

Having a clear idea of what style, or combination of styles, you desire will allow the creative process to focus on the materials you need, to make your true inspiration a reality.

Organize Your Thoughts

Chapter 2

Take a survey of your rooms and ask yourself:

DOES THE ROOM LACK LIGHT? – Knowing this helps with the placement of furnishings and lighting fixtures.

WHAT COLORS DO I LOVE/HATE? – It will help in giving you a direction in the design process.

WHAT DO I LOVE ABOUT THIS ROOM? – What you love about the room could become the focal point that you'll use to design the room.

WHAT DO I DISLIKE ABOUT THIS ROOM? – It

will give you a clear idea of what you want replaced.

IS THE ROOM TOO NARROW? – Being conscious of the dimensions of your room will help in deciding on the color scheme, décor, and furnishings you'll use.

DO THE FURNISHINGS CLASH? – This realization will help you avoid the same mistakes during the design process.

DO I HAVE A SPECIFIC STYLE I WANT TO CREATE? – If you're not sure, research rooms. Recognize the characteristics and trend that you're most attracted to: the style of the décor, quality, and quantity of furniture, patterns, colors, materials, etc. Let those characteristics guide you and go with your gut!

WHAT IS MY BUDGET? – Not knowing your budget could leave your project unfinished and could lead to stress and unhappiness.

Boards are great tools for organizing thoughts and ideas. Once you've identified the theme you want for your home, write it on the board along with glued-on pictures of examples of how you would like your home to look. Google the keyword corresponding to the theme of your home and simply print out the pictures and images that catch your attention. Pictures can also be found on design magazines, Pinterest, and several other outlets. If you're feeling very creative, you can also draw your own pictures.

In the following chapters, you will find everything you need to learn to decorate and organize your home. The subjects will range from how to find furniture bargains to how to design each room of your home. Each section has been clearly labeled for your convenience, to make it easier for you to come back to a specific section after you have completed the book.

"Life is a journey," they say, but designing and decorating your home is a journey too! I encourage you to take before and after pictures so that you can proudly assess how far you've come in your designing journey while you bask in the glory of the end results.

Furnishings

Chapter 3

When it comes to furnishing your home, or space, it is not necessary to go shopping for the most expensive furniture. It is possible to find bargains, or even DIY your own furniture and décor!

Bargains

Bargains can be found in the form of "End of Season" sales, "Holiday" sales, and store coupons when available. Many people are unaware that, in some instances, the customer does not have to pay full price for furniture and a small percentage will be taken off the tag price if the object one wants to buy has some kind of imperfection such as a scratch, smudge or tear. So, start inspecting your furniture and ask for a bargain!

Also, have you ever wondered what happens to "old" furniture when hotels remodel? You haven't? Well, let me tell you; most of them don't just discard their (sometimes barely used) furniture. Instead, they sell them to liquidators who sell them to the general public at really low prices.

Make sure you look for liquidators in your area.

DIY

Find a garage sale or visit your local thrift shop, because you might come across your next DIY project. There are multitudes of videos online and on YouTube on how to DIY anything from a bedpost to a wall display. If you want to be a savvy interior designer—and save some major bucks, I might add—make full use of outlets such as YouTube. I assure that this resource will add to your project.

Décor

Décor brings life to a room; it is an expression of your personality, and it tells people who you are. Make the best impression by searching and learning about the materials that will aid you in making your home "uniquely you".

Fashion for Your Walls

You don't have money to hire a painter to paint your walls? Who said you need one? You can paint the walls yourself! You don't care for the mess and the time painting requires? Don't worry, be happy! You can use other material to bring life to your walls.

Wallpaper is a great alternative to paint. The days of "Grandma–style" wallpapers are over, and you can find nice, modern wallpaper at most hardware stores and online. One can find a plethora of colors, textures, patterns, and finishes to choose from. The most popular are:

COATED FABRIC – fabric wallpaper is durable and washable, it is also "breathable", which makes it ideal for use in areas such as the living room. However, it does not typically come pre-pasted and it is a bit harder to work with.

VINYL COATED PAPER – this type of wallpaper is the least expensive, but it is also easily stained and difficult to clean.

PAPER BACKED VINYL – works well in every area of the home and it comes pre-pasted.

SOLID VINYL – is usually laminated to a fabric or paper substrate. It is considered more durable than coated fabric wallpapers because, in addition to being washable, it can be scrubbed.

FIBERGLASS WEAVES – this type of wallpaper is extremely durable, it can adhere to concrete and brick, and is mostly used in commercial settings. It is extremely difficult to peel off once it's been exposed to moisture. I do not typically recommend this type of wallpaper for places of residence.

The above is not a comprehensive list, it is

merely a breakdown of the widely used wallpapers.

Renters can also get in on the wallpaper action with removable/self-adhesive wallpaper and other such materials. With the large availability of removable products, now renters can also transform their spaces into glamorous homes without jeopardizing their security deposit.

SELF-ADHESIVE/REMOVABLE WALLPAPER – or Tempaper, is designed to peel off easily when needed, making it an ideal alternative for apartment renters. Like regular wallpaper, it comes in a variety of colors, styles, and patterns. Some plain, white, self-adhesive wallpaper can also be painted and will protect the surface underneath.

CONTACT PAPER AND SELF-ADHESIVE SHELF LINER – can also be used to fashion your walls. It is very easy to apply and is very inexpensive.

WALL DECALS – they come in different shapes, sizes, words and, when used tastefully, they can accentuate a wall. When arranged in a continuous pattern, wall decals can even replace paint and wallpaper. They are easier to manage and take less time to apply. They also are a great way to express your personality and bring a bit of uniqueness to your room. Wall decals can be used in virtually every room of your home; all you need to do to ensure that they will stick is to prep your wall by making sure that it's clean and dry.

PEEL-AND-STICK TILE SHEETS – are a great way to create a backsplash and they can be found at some of the most popular hardware stores. They are easy to install, and can be removed by the simple use of a hair dryer.

DUCK TAPE AND SELF-ADHESIVE STRIPES – they are a great decorative technique, and, like wall decals, they stick easily and remove cleanly and allow you to achieve any design or pattern. They are commonly used to give the illusion of width and depth. Horizontal stripes make a room appear more spacious; vertical stripes make the ceiling appear higher. I would suggest using them on a single wall to make it a feature wall.

It is important to be mindful about the role colors play in the illusion of space in your room. Warm hues—reds, oranges, and yellows—tend to pull walls together, hence creating the illusion of a smaller space. For example, if you paint a wall bright red, it will seem closer to you than a white wall. Cool colors—blues, greens, and purples—have the opposite effect of warm hues as it is possible to create the illusion of a longer or wider room. (Tip: Colors do their jobs even better if used for a feature, or accent, wall) Make sure to pick the right walls when you attempt to shorten, narrow, widen, or heighten the walls. Pick a wall that can tolerate being "fore-shortened" like this, perhaps the farthest or longest wall in the room. So, according to this theory, painting a side wall red can make a room feel too narrow, but painting an end wall in a long, narrow room will make the room feel more balanced in size.

Wall Accessories

Paintings are a great way to accessorize your wall, but you don't have to settle for expensive, store-bought art. Once again, the internet comes to the rescue! There is a wide array of DIY tutorials for creating anything from decorative mirrors to paintings. Check out Pinterest, Instagram, or YouTube and be inspired!

"Fake It 'til You Make It" Room Décor

One of the most popular ways to add a bit of chic to your room is with the use of flowers. However, if you don't want to spend money every week buying fresh, new flowers that only last a couple of days, you can use the alternative: faux flowers and plants. Nowadays it is possible—and easy—to find realistic artificial flowers, and then all you need to do is make a nice arrangement. Buy a vase, some artificial flowers, and simulated water—or artificial water—at a craft store. Just follow the directions on the simulated water box; there are also some tutorials on YouTube. Who needs a florist?

Now that I have presented you with the vast possibilities and choices you have at your disposal to furnish and decorate your home, the next chapters will provide you with an in-depth look at how to design each of your rooms.

The Foyer

Chapter 4

The foyer, or hallway, is the first thing that a person sees after they enter your front door, and it is your chance to set the tone for the rest of your home. The foyer is a "passing through room", and although there is no need to invest as much time in this room as the rest of the rooms, there are ways in which you can set a welcoming mood.

WALLS AND DÉCOR – If you want your entrance to say, "Welcome, please come in," use warm, vibrant colors, which convey joy and ease.

ACCESSORIES – flowers and tastefully arranged wall décor are great ways to catch your guests' interest immediately. For small spaces, a large mirror is the way to go to create the illusion of extra room. If space allows, I would also suggest tucking a small chair and table (or simply just a chair) in a corner to create a cozier feel. As the final touch that ties your foyer together, consider placing an aisle runner on the floor. However, make sure the aisle runner is a good length away from the door to prevent a mess every time it is opened.

The Living Room

Chapter 5

The living room is the entertainment spot of the house. It is the place where you gather with your family, where you receive guests, and spend some "me time" while you binge-watch the latest Netflix show. There are several things you need to ask yourself before decorating your living room—and you should write them down on the board as well:

1. WHAT IS THE FUNCTION OF THE ROOM? – will you use it to study/read? Will it serve as an occasional dining spot?

2. WHO WILL BE USING THE ROOM? – do you live alone? Do you have a partner? Any children? Older persons?

Pets? (For a room to be effective, the potential needs of all must be considered)

3. HOW OFTEN WILL THE ROOM BE USED? – occasional or daily use?
4. IS THERE A NEED FOR STORAGE? – e.g. storing electrical items, books, toys, collectible items, etc.
5. IS LIGHTING IMPORTANT? – for reading, entertainment, etc.

These are only some of the basic questions you need to consider when designing your space, because planning and analyzing the function of a room is the most important step to get what you truly want and need.

Design Style

It takes a few seconds for a person to evaluate another when they first meet; this is what we call "First impression". People form opinions of one another based on appearance, demeanor, and body language. The living room is viewed as the first impression of your home because, although the foyer is often what your guest sees first, they spend merely seconds in that space; the living room is the place where your guest will spend most of his visit. Make sure you showcase your style and personality in the living room. The following is a short list of possible living room styles.

CALM: the feel of stillness can be accomplished by selecting neutral colors for furniture and décor, which can be tied in with white walls or other light tone, relaxing colors.

ROMANTIC: can be accomplished with the use of light fabrics such as sheer and silk. Velvet pillows, crystal, silver, and gold accents will add a touch of glamour to your room.

ELEGANT: just like the romantic room, elegance can be accomplished by the use of crystal, silver, and gold décor. However, elegance does not need to be flashy! The simple use of curved furniture (e.g., sofas and chairs) and silk can give the room a refined feel.

DRAMATIC: can be created by the use of red, black and white walls (e.g., stripes) or one bold feature wall. Also, keep the room clutter free and open with a conservative amount of furniture and décor.

MASCULINE: use traditional dark colors for the walls and furniture. However, introduce a brighter color in the form of wall décor and furniture décor.

Tip: Be mindful of the amount of light available in your room (how many windows do you have? How much sunlight does your room receive? How many light fixtures and where are they placed?). Keep in mind that lighting also plays a big part in your design.

The Kitchen

Chapter 6

Kitchens are often said to be the heart of the house, and I've yet to find that to be untrue. There we cook, we eat, we entertain, and spend time with our families. When decorating and designing this important part of the house, think about the way you currently use your kitchen. Analyzing how you use this space, or how you would like to use it, will help you maximize its potential.

Cabinets

While keeping in mind your design style, decide what you intend to do to update the kitchen cabinets. At times, just changing your hardware can do wonders to your cabinets. Other times, the way to go is to replace the cabinets but, if you're on a budget, you might want to consider repainting them with a fresh new coat of paint or a brand new color.

The following is a short list of recommended colors for your cabinets:

NATURA COLORS – white, beige, and browns are the most popular and work well with most wallpaper and wall colors.

BRIGHT COLORS AND PASTEL COLORS – colors such as yellow and turquoise can energize the kitchen and give it a sense of uniqueness. When going this route, I suggest keeping the walls white to avoid overwhelming feelings.

DUAL COLORS – an innovative way to design your cabinets is to paint the upper cabinets a different color than the lower cabinets. For sophistication, try a combination of black and white, and for fun a bright color at the bottom and a neutral hue at the top.

OPEN SHELVING – If you decide to go with

open shelving, line the back of the shelves with wallpaper to create an eye-catching decorative touch, or simply paint them in an unexpected color.

Painting your cabinets is a great way to showcase your style and personality while refreshing your kitchen. However, if you decide to go this route make sure to visit your local hardware store and ask about and research cabinet painting material and the right methods for using them.

The Alternative to Painting Cabinets

Renters are not always able to paint kitchen cabinets, but they can still get in on the cabinet "revamp" action without jeopardizing their security deposits. Self-adhesive wallpaper, or contact paper, is a great alternative to painting cabinets and stylizing kitchen appliances. It will take some patience to apply, but it will remove cleanly when it's time to move at the end of your lease.

Walls

When painting the kitchen walls, red, yellow, and white are some of the best colors. Red is said to be an appetite stimulant, which makes sense in view of this room's function. Furthermore, red is a color that "pops", which is great if you're looking to make a statement. Yellow is a happy and soothing color, and will help give the illusion of space to a small kitchen. The freshness and cleanliness of white will go well with any type of cabinet color and wall décor.

To create a sophisticated and enhanced look, also consider adding a backsplash in the sink and stove top area walls—renters should purchase peel-n-stick alternatives.

Décor

Wall paintings, flowers, and chalkboards are just some of the accessories that will give beauty and style to this heavily used space. Pinterest provides a plethora of kitchen decoration ideas and tips.

Organization

Organization in this heavily trafficked room is important. No one wants a cluttered, disorganized kitchen. Dinnerware, plates, and knives should be in close proximity to the dishwasher or sink, so as to make storage of these everyday items quick and easy. Additional utensils, such as wooden spoons, can be arranged bouquet-style in a nice canister or mason jar. Free up counter space by placing the microwave on a shelf where possible, and by condensing appliances, such as blenders and toasters, in a specific area. If you don't have cabinet space for your pots and pans or other kitchen essentials, consider the purchase of freestanding racks or furniture.

The
Dining Room

Chapter 7

The dining room is another place of food consumption and social gatherings, but sometimes it is also used as workspace and a place to do homework. The success of a well-designed dining room lies in planning and knowing how the room will be used.

Furniture

A generously sized table is ready to provide room for anything ranging from holiday dinners to workspace, but it is up to you to decide which kind of table will cater to your needs. A round table works best for informal dinners as it sits more people. On the other hand, square tables only work for four people. However, you can correct the problem by buying a square table that extends to a rectangle. Whatever shape you select, make sure to be mindful of the space you have and consider whether you will be able to walk around the table and pull out a chair easily. Both wood and glass topped tables are good for the dining room but keep in mind that glass tables increase the feeling of space.

Dining rooms are also a great place to have credenzas and buffet credenzas. Dining rooms that are extensions of the living room are great for having big, or small, bars to really entertain the guests. Now that's a party!

In apartments where space is limited, use a small table and position it by the window. If you're really inspired, you could also create a counter top at right angles to the walls that can fold away.

Color

This room is often in the kitchen or attached to the living room. When the dining room is a continuation of another room, make sure to design it as an extension of that room. In those instances in which the dining room is a standalone room, the ideal wall colors should be similar to the color palettes suggested for the kitchen.

Décor

To keep the dining room modern and cool, place a large rug under the dining set and use light window treatments to let natural light in—where windows are available.

The kind of accessories used for the living room also work well in the dining room. Also, hanging a large painting, or other large wall decoration, works very well in the dining room.

The dining room is the easiest room to design and decorate; if you follow these simple principles and tips, the result will be a stunning room no matter what you do to it.

The Bedroom

Chapter 8

The bedroom is the place we go to relax and recharge from the stressors of our everyday life. The bedroom is also a loving place where we share the most intimate parts of ourselves. The kitchen is the heart of the house, but the bedroom is the sanctuary and should be treated as such and, like the rest of the house, it should highlight our personality to make it feel just right.

Design Style and Color

Designing the bedroom is totally up to you! And you can use the same design styles used in the Living Room section of this guide. However, if you intend to use your bedroom only for relaxation purposes, I suggest the colors addressed in the calm style. If your goal is to relax, I would definitely stay away from strong colors, such as red, because they are too stimulating.

Furniture

There is a wide array of bedroom furniture styles out there, and some you can do yourself (e.g., DIY bedroom headboard), but there are 3 basic pieces that should be part of your room no matter the style you choose:

THE BED – for obvious reasons, the bed is the single most important thing in the room. Since the bed occupies the most room, the size is very important. When buying the bed consider who will be using it. Are you single? Do you have a partner? Do you like the mattress firm or soft? Are you considering a headboard and footboard? No matter what size or comfort level you choose, remember to measure both the bed—including headboard and footboard—and the area size before purchase.

THE NIGHTSTAND – They come in different

shapes, styles and colors, they look good, and they help tie the room together. Also, you'll be able to keep lamps, electronics, and reading material in hands' reach. If you regularly share your bed with someone else, it is usual to have a nightstand on each side of the bed, but if you are single, you can get away with having a single nightstand.

THE DRESSER – besides looking nice, dressers serve as storage. Dressers' storage capacity ranges anywhere from a simple three-drawer to a nine-drawer design. Same as when shopping for a bed, consider the space you have available when purchasing a dresser.

Décor

If you have a single night stand, you can balance the lack on the other side of the bed, with a free standing lamp or a decorative chair.

For a more polished look, when considering a rug under the bed, make sure you line the beginning of the rug with the nightstand, or you can line the rug with the back of the nightstand and bed. Not lining the rug correctly could make the room look a bit "off".

Accessorize the room the way you like best. I suggest candles, flowers, and wall art. However, a well-made bed, with lots of pillows—regular and decorative—can be enough to make the room look cozy. Curtains are also a personal, and mostly physical, choice: If you are a morning person and like to feel energized, hanging light curtains allows the natural morning light to infiltrate the room and gently wake you up. However, if you have trouble sleeping, opt for a dark shade curtain to avoid lights during sleep.

Storage

In the bedroom, we keep all our garments and personal possessions, but we often lack the necessary space. If you don't have drawers as part of your bed frame, you can purchase under bed storage boxes. Another way to maximize the storage capacity in the room is to consider a chest, or storage ottoman, at the foot of the bed, and closet organizers. Keeping clutter to a minimum will avoid distractions and the uneasiness that untidiness causes, and it will, most importantly, create the atmosphere of calmness that you are trying to achieve.

The Bathroom

Chapter 9

The bathroom is one of the most important rooms of the home. There we relax, and take care of ourselves. It is a sort of "safe haven" and we should devote more time to making it as accommodating as possible.

Atmosphere

One of the first things to consider in a bathroom is color and light. To give the illusion of space, even in smaller bathrooms, consider cool colored walls. If you're lucky enough to have windows in your bathrooms, be sure to make good use of the natural light by choosing curtains or shades that are light and sheer. Similarly, artificial lighting can be your friend in the creation of brightness and space. By placing lights beside and below the sink and shower, you can create a feeling of height and depth—not to mention what lights can do for the creation of a relaxing, or even romantic, ambiance in the bathroom.

Walls

Another way to add dimension is with the choice you make for your walls. Vertical or horizontal stripes (self-adhesive stripes or wallpaper for renters) will add a sense of height or depth to the entire space. Besides making a bold statement, a feature wall, or accent wall, can also be used as an asset for dimension. By the use of cool colors—blues, greens and purples—you can make a short room seem longer, or a narrow room feel wider.

Décor

Invite flowers (or DIY artificial arrangements) into your bathroom; it will make the room feel more inviting and accommodating. If used tastefully, picture frames, candles, and accent décor can also increase the quality of your bathroom. To give your bathroom a dash of elegance, consider attaching an extra rod to your bathtub and placing window curtains over it. It's Instaglamour! (See Pinterest for examples)

Storage

Besides being decorative, hanging wicker baskets on the bathroom wall can provide storage for towels, tissues, soap, magazines, bath toys, etc. Extra storage can also be accomplished by placing shelves and hooks in the spaces beside the vanity, behind the door, or over the toilet. Shelving, hanging baskets, and hooks provide convenient storage without intruding on floor space.

The Laundry Room

Chapter 10

The laundry room does not need to be a secluded room where you only go to wash your dirty socks. Like the rest of your home, it needs to be pleasant and comfortable, and the following suggestions will aid you in making the best out of your laundry room.

Maximize the Space

Often, laundry rooms are small, and the best way to add some extra space is to stack the dryer on top of the washer. Just make sure that you have a front-loading washing machine. The extra space could be used to add a storage cabinet—or a place to hide your hamper with dirty clothes—fold out drying racks, or a small station table to fold your laundry.

Another way to maximize your laundry space, and reduce clutter, is to use the space behind the door to hang clothes, or laundry items. This can be accomplished with the purchase of door racks and hooks.

Color

Light colors work best for the walls and furniture of your laundry room, because light and bright colors elevate the spirits, and we know we could use a good mood while we're doing the daunting task of washing, ironing/steaming, and folding the laundry.

Lighting

Lighting in the laundry room is important. If you are not lucky enough to have windows and natural lights, you can make up for it by installing wall and under cabinet lighting.

Tip: To avoid extra wires, and extra work, consider purchasing battery operated lights. They are inexpensive and a great alternative for renters.

Décor

To create a cool environment, consider backsplash and floor tiles for your laundry room (peel-n-stick alternative for renters). You could also add a nice throw rug on the floor and some laundry-inspired wall art.

Tip: Check out Pinterest for DIY laundry room décor.

The Balcony

Chapter 11

When decorating, remember to give your balcony as much attention as the rest of your home, because this space can add style and a peaceful atmosphere to your home. During the warm weather months, your balcony can be used as a second living room and a great "outdoorsy" entertainment spot.

Furniture

To create a comfy sitting area, all you need is a small couch, bench, or simply use trunks and place cushions and pillows on top of them. Trunks are great because they can double as storage for your pillows, throws, and accessories. Also, a trunk can also be used as a decorative center table.

Tip: If you are on a tight budget, use crate boxes instead of trunks. You can paint them to match your décor.

Décor

Bare balconies can be simply decorated with flowers and other plants. However, to showcase your style, make sure you incorporate your favorite fabrics and colors by adding pillow cushions and rugs—alternatives to rugs are rubber mats—and for the creation of a romantic or mystical environment at night, consider hanging string lights and lanterns.

Tip: If you live in an apartment, and your balcony faces the street or neighbor's home, you can create some privacy by putting up material such as bamboo screens or Roman blinds.

Another Word from the Author

The ultimate aim, when designing and decorating your home, is to have fun! The rest will fall into place. This short guide provided you with an easy and clear look at how to tackle design and decorating projects in every room of your home. At the end of this book, if you're still not motivated enough to decorate your space ... well, hire me!

Jokes aside, decorating your home is a rewarding experience that can help you discover the creative abilities that you didn't know you had. My hope is that, during this reading journey, you were able to come up with some ideas that will help you in the creation of a home that is unique, beautiful, and evokes joy within you and within all who step foot in it.

About the Author

Grace Annan is a social worker, author, interior designer, wedding planner, event planner, and entrepreneur. She likes learning about different things, and thinks of herself as eclectic and not having to conform to the norm of settling for one single profession.

She was born and raised in Italy but her parents are originally from Ghana, West Africa.

Grace Annan currently lives in Florida.

Made in the USA
Lexington, KY
14 March 2019